Visions of
Reason

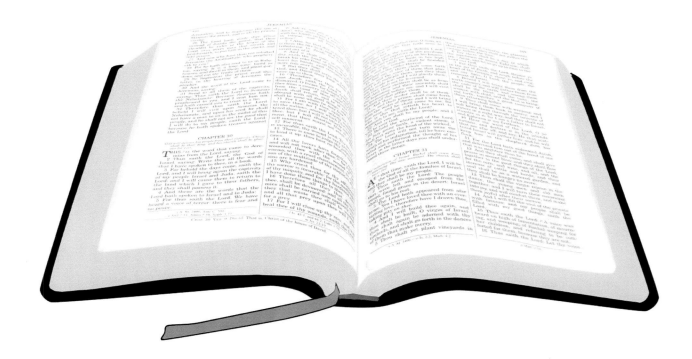

JACOB BUTKIEWICZ

To order additional copies of this book, contact:
Xlibris
844-714-8691
www.Xlibris.com
Orders@Xlibris.com

ISBN: Softcover   978-1-7960-3638-1
        EBook   978-1-7960-3637-4

Print information available on the last page

Rev. date: 05/03/2024

1. Your smile can go a long way.

2. Christ Blood binds our Love together.

3. Don't run away from the Promise Christ has intended for you.

4. Sometimes in order to get the desired outcome you have to go through adversity.

5. We do better if we roll together.

6. Every person has an approach & Jesus is the only one that can go about each of us the right way.

7. Football Linemen train hard during the offseason; similar to being a Christian, by accepting Christ were encouraged through prayer, scripture, and fellowship to hold the line for the Lord.

8. Its selfish for us to say were alone to God who told us not to be simple.

9. When the devil tells you things in your head that go's contrary to the Doctrine of what Christ has said, "Don't Listen".

10. When the devil causes shame, sadness, regrets, negative edges of emotions, bring those ill feelings to the Lord.

11. Your not bound by the enemy but held tight by the Lord.

Ephesians 5:20

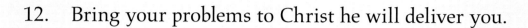

12. Bring your problems to Christ he will deliver you.

13. Christ wants you to individually expand on all the things that are True & Good.

14. Rain falling cleanses the Body & Earth; similar to Forgiveness, Christ Love & Mercy washes us Free of sin.

15. Surrounded by darkness the Lord picks you up.

16. When anyone talks to you, you got to look at their whole dialogue, it will show you many things.

17. It says a lot when someone has your back.

18. Evil in numbers underestimates the perseverance of those who seek the true Glory in Jesus Christ.

19. The Lords thoughts go beyond our imaginations.

20. The Lord makes sense through everything.

21. May Christ name always Reign with His Glory.

Deuteronomy 31:6

22. The Faucet in the bathtub is turned providing Hot or Cold water; similar to discernment, the direction of one's mind, runs to be filled by the choices between Good & Evil.

23. Nothing can withhold the might of God.

24. Christ is hope for all.

25. Be thankful you are you and not someone else.

26. The Lord gives us more meaning.

27. I want to be there for people like Christ was there for me.

28. Only through the resolutions of Christ may my Destiny be set free.

29. Creator & Creation you can't take God out of Life.

30. Mans simple Bread doesn't last long compared to Bread of Life found in Christ.

31. You can't deny people in Christ if Christ didn't deny you.

32. No one should have to wander to find Love.

Matthew 5:43-44

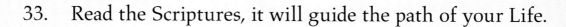

33. Read the Scriptures, it will guide the path of your Life.

34. If God can do Good for Us, Love Us, and gave us His Son Jesus, then we can emulate that Goodness unto others and spread Christ Love onto all.

35. The Lord fulfills His commitments.

36. With Christ, "I'm still standing."

37. Stop looking at me as the problem & turn towards Christ as the solution.

38. Through Christ were going to do it together.

39. Lord you're my all.

40. Christ looks to keep us together while the enemy uses sin to divide us apart.

41. Jesus Christ is the Best.

42. Let Christ be the center of all are Life's attachments.

43. I always have hope, because the Love of Christ gives me that Hope.

1 John 4:7-8

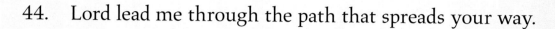

44. Lord lead me through the path that spreads your way.

45. Christ can bring all paths to turn towards his direction.

46. The Lord makes it all count.

47. In Christ name & His gain.

48. Lord anew me.

49. Never would have been the same if I didn't have the Lord to call on.

50. God willed a way to create us & through His Son Jesus brought us to Him.

51. Lord let every Non-believer find that Joy that every Christian has found in you.

52. What you see fit for me Lord that's what I seek in you.

53. Through Christ there is no end.

54. You can always look back at their smile.

1 John 4:10

55. Nothing satisfies the emptiness unless you find that wholeness through Christ.

56. Through Christ Mercy Let His Love Reign.

57. Let Jesus name be the Remedy.

58. When we seek the Lord he gives us our completions.

59. Lord I pray you bring every name to you.

60. Let no name Lord be forgotten.

61. In your time Lord.

62. Lord teach me always to get back up for more.

63. Darkness is primitive.

64. Through thick and thin your there Lord.

65. Not everybody gives you that time.

Revelation 2:7

66. Christ purpose is necessary.

67. Lord set the course for your direction.

68. The Lord set the table, Let us all sit with Him.

69. You ever wonder what's going on in other star systems & how its effecting Earth and how we are effecting them?

70. We might not see Eye to Eye but the Lords Love and Mercy that has brought us together.

71. Let Christ voice guide the flock as we all move towards Him.

72. Everything about you Lord is the thing to do.

73. Christ wants you.

74. Your Love Lord is what we need.

75. Let your heart never wander the Lords Love is always with you.

76. Everybody has a special purpose, something within that separates us in a positive way.

Ephesians 6:11

77. I Love Seeing Brothers & Sisters come together strengthening the bonds & building what Christ intended for.

78. When you include Christ he covers everything.

79. What can we do to help further Christ as our Cause?

80. Christ Love can break through any Boundary or Blockade.

81. The Lords Love brings us together.

82. We go further with Love and nowhere with hate.

83. When you Brighten someone's Day it's like a Candle being lit to further keep the darkness away.

84. Giving Alms to the poor is what Christ does for all of Us in Spirit, by restoring wholeness to the just.

85. Christ Brings us Unity.

86. Appreciate your dreams each one is a gift.

87. Just Living Lord Everyday You give me hope.

88. The Hope you see in Christ is the Life He sees in you.

John 3:16

89. Jesus knows what it takes.

90. Christ brings out the Best in Us.

91. Present all your supplications to the Lord & He will guide your steps.

92. If Christ can forgive us of our faults then we can look past each others.

93. The Lord moves you on the board Trust Him to deliver your pieces to Victory.

94. We all stand for something.

95. Lord you heal all my sicknesses.

96. If we keep striving to do better you'll get better.

97. God doesn't make junk.

98. The Lord will reassure you with the answers you need.

99. We get to see how special we are to one another when we come around to each other.

John 14:6

100. All you need to do to accept Jesus as your Lord and Savior is ask him into your heart & that he would forgive you of your sins.

1 John 3:2

Special Thanks

I wanted to thank the Lord for all that he has done for me throughout my Life. I want to thank my parents for raising me right and instilling everything they had into to me growing up. I want to thank my grandparents for always loving and supporting me. I want to thank my family for always showing Love and supporting me. Thank you to my fellow veterans that I served with and have met thank you for always being a Brother or Sister to me. I want to thank all the people that have been there for me I appreciate you all. I want to thank JRaphael Edmundo Honasan for the Artwork. I Love you God and thank you for everything.

If you like this book, you may also check other books author
has written:

The Book of Sayings

The Color of Wisdom

Arts of Truth

The Ant Who Found The Truth

Printed in the United States
by Baker & Taylor Publisher Services